MY BIBLE stories
Activity Book

Turn the page to discover inspirational
Bible stories and exciting puzzles and activities.

•

Then press out the card pages to create
some fantastic Bible-themed crafts.

•

You can use your puffy stickers in the book,
to finish your crafts, or wherever else you want!

make
believe
ideas

GOD'S CREATION

God made the world and everything in it.
He made the sun to shine during the day.
Circle six differences between the two pictures of God's creation.

NIGHT LIFE

God made the moon and the stars to glow at night.
Trace the lines to finish the scene. Then color it.

3

GARDEN MAZE

God made Adam and Eve, and they lived in the Garden of Eden. A snake tempted them to eat the forbidden fruit. Help Adam and Eve avoid the snakes and guide them to the apple tree.

Start →

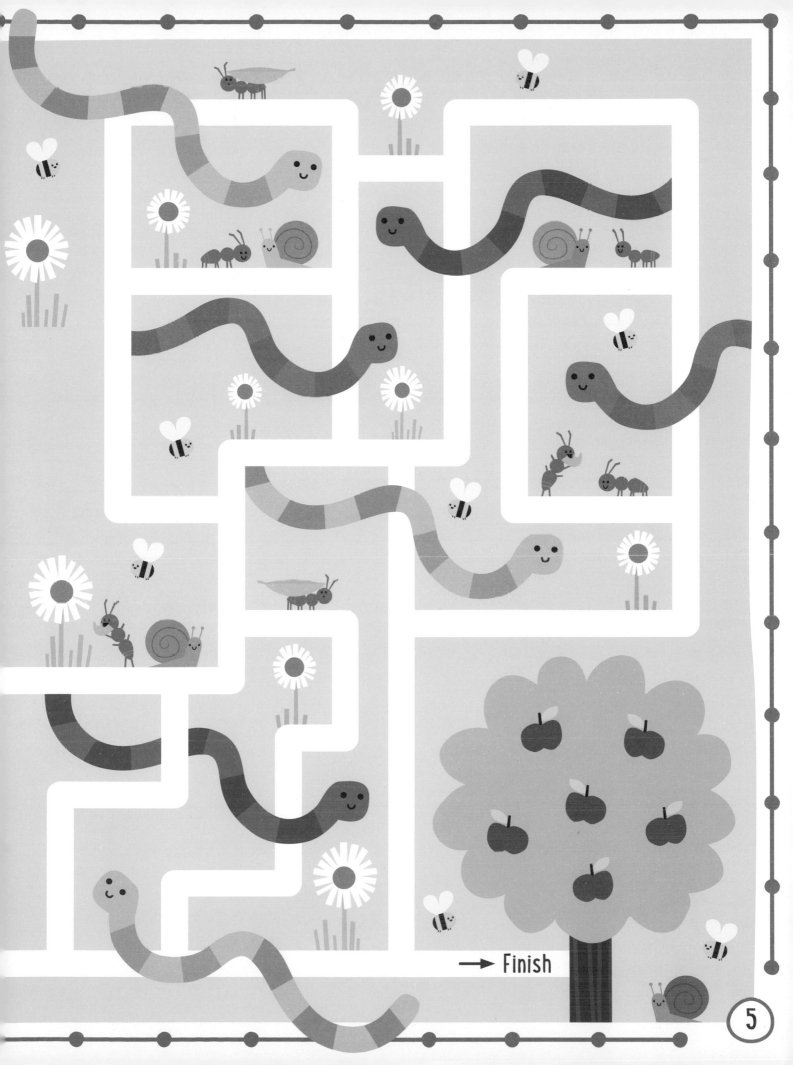

→ Finish

5

NOAH'S SEARCH

God told Noah to build a big boat called an ark.
Search the grid to help Noah find the animals he must keep safe.

lion

monkey

frog

snake

giraffe

penguin

f	m	o	r	i	u	h	t	a	p
r	r	e	t	g	x	s	m	d	z	e
h	x	i	s	n	a	k	e	n	n
a	z	g	n	h	o	t	s	y	g
m	u	w	j	p	d	g	u	q	u
o	y	l	s	a	j	x	l	h	i
n	r	i	f	f	v	f	r	k	n
k	q	o	m	h	f	r	o	g	u
e	f	n	c	e	n	k	w	i	k
y	b	e	g	i	r	a	f	f	e

OCEAN SHADOWS

God sent a terrible storm. Noah sailed for 40 days and nights.
Draw lines to match the sea creatures to the correct-shaped shadow.

COLOR THE RAINBOW

The rain stopped and God sent a beautiful rainbow.
Color the rainbow. Use the dots to guide you.

COUNT THE ANIMALS

Noah and the animals were kept safe by God.
Help Noah count his animals to finish the sums.

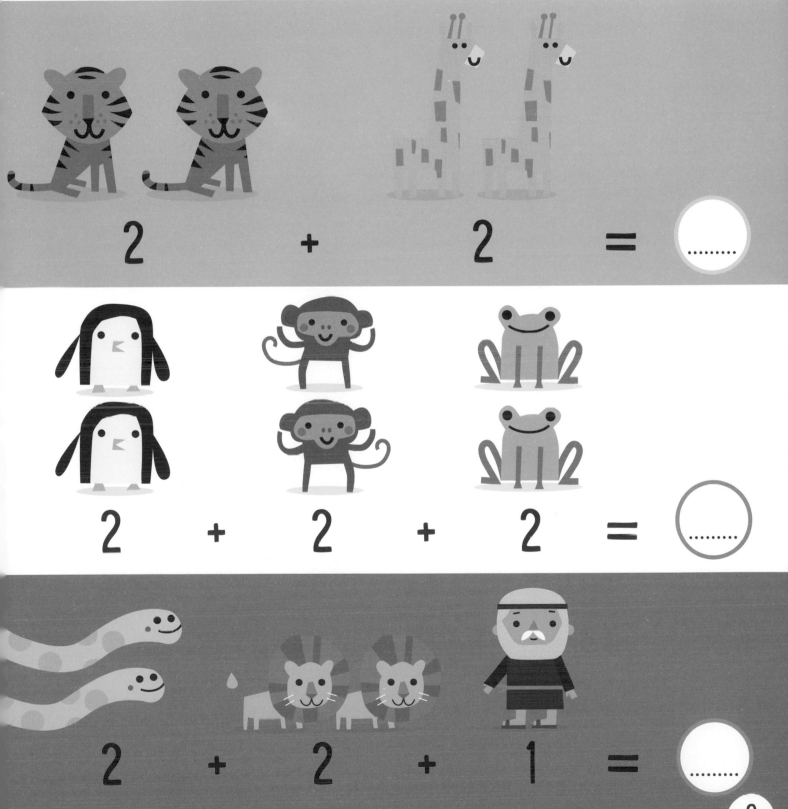

2   +   2   = ...

2   +   2   +   2   = ...

2   +   2   +   1   = ...

COLORFUL COAT

Joseph was given a colorful coat as a gift from his father. Joseph's brothers were jealous. Search the scene for the things below.

Circle the sheep that matches this shape.

PRISON BREAK

Joseph's brothers sold him to merchants, who put him in prison in Egypt. Guide Joseph through the prison to help him escape.

Start →

→ Finish

COUNT THE CORN

The King of Egypt asked Joseph to help people store food for the famine. Count the baskets of corn in each column, and then write the totals in the circles.

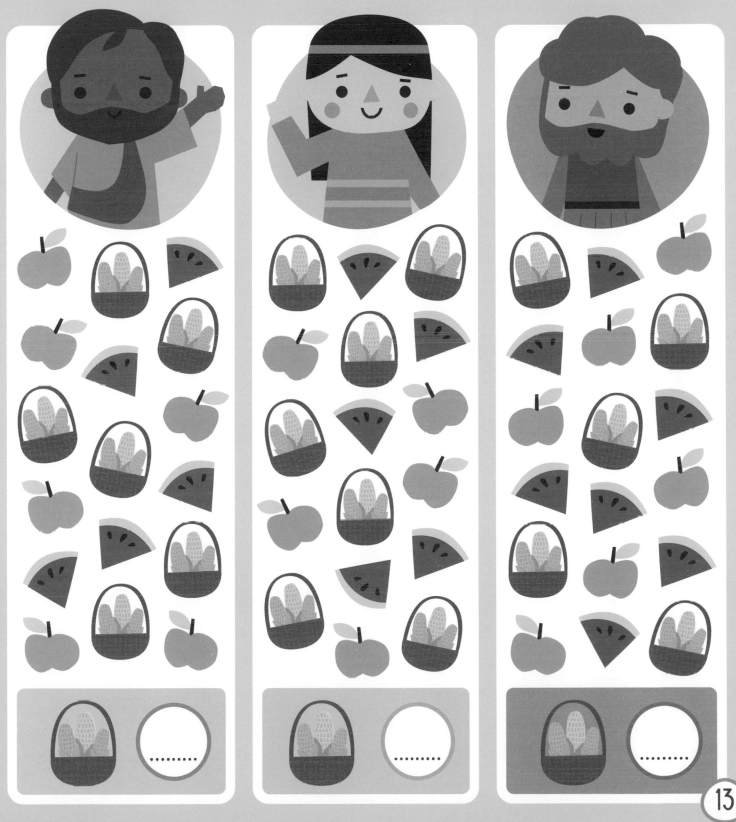

BABY MOSES

An Egyptian princess found baby Moses in a basket by the river.
Circle **true** for the things that are in the picture.
Circle **false** for the things that are not in the picture.

Baby Moses is in a basket.	True	False
The water in the river is green.	True	False
The camel has one hump.	True	False

PARTING THE SEA

God helped Moses to part the Red Sea and lead His people out of slavery in Egypt.
Join the dots to draw Moses. Then color him.

COUNT DAVID'S SHEEP

David was a brave shepherd boy who protected his sheep. Help David count his sheep and write the answer. ➝ ....

GOLIATH THE GIANT

Goliath was a tall and strong soldier who was fighting David's people. Color the picture. Use the key to guide you.

Key: 1 2 3 4 5 6

DAVID FIGHTS GOLIATH

David was not afraid of Goliath and fought him until the giant fell.
Search the battle for the things below.

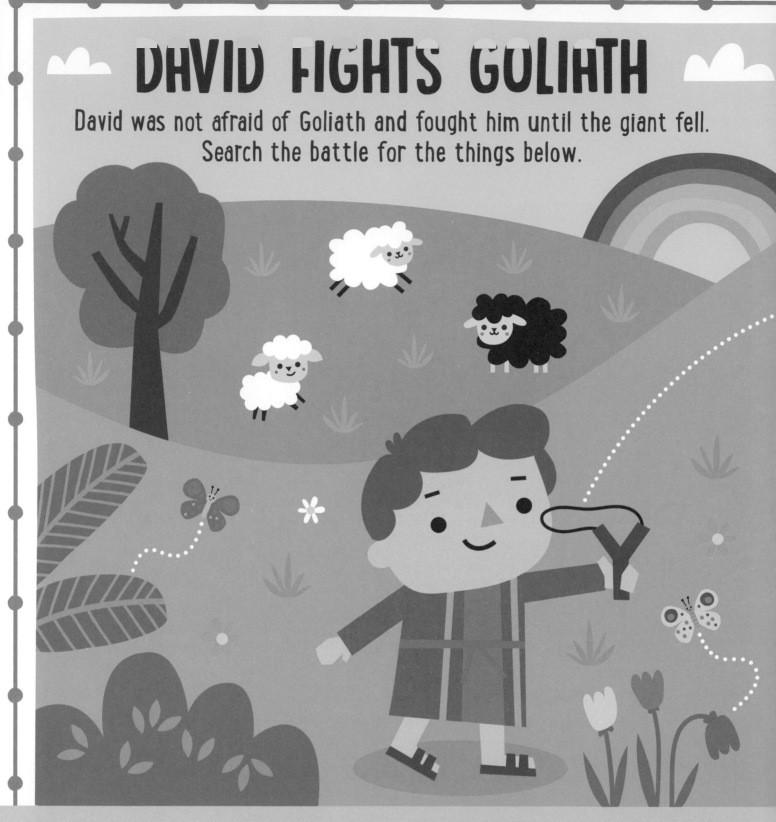

Check the boxes as you find them.

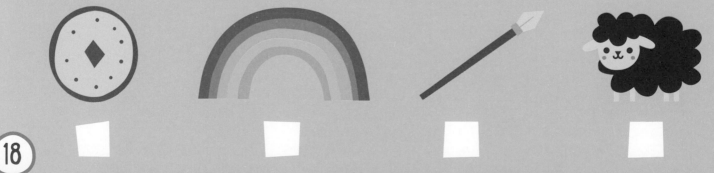

DANIEL AND THE LIONS

Daniel prayed to God every day. Enemies arrested Daniel and threw him into the lions' den. Unscramble the words. Use the pictures as a guide.

s o n l i

_ _ _ _ _

n a e r D l i

_ _ _ _ _ _

The law said you could only pray to the king.
Color the picture of Daniel praying.

LION ART

Copy the lion. Use the grid to guide you.

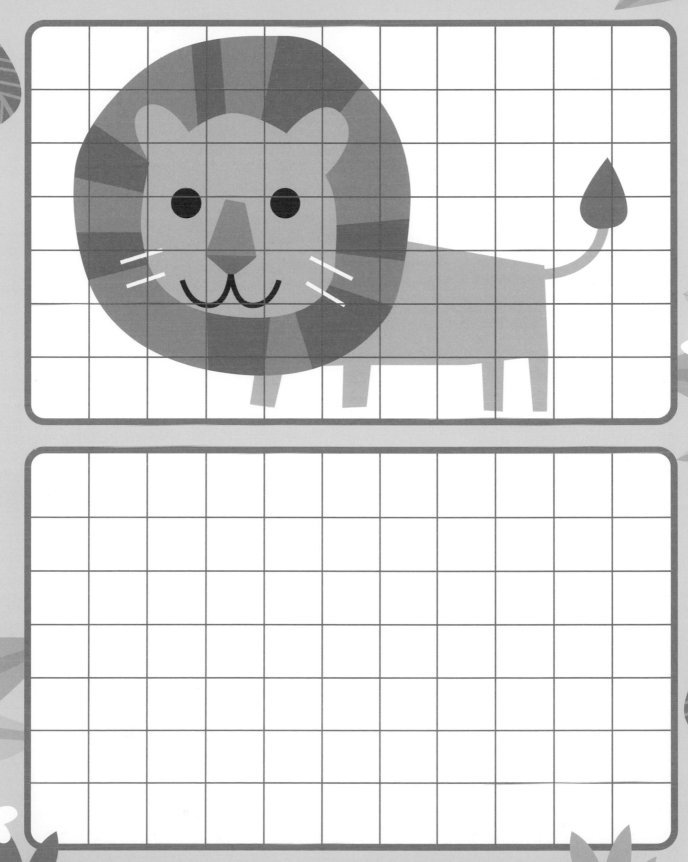

LIONS' DEN

God kept Daniel safe in the lions' den. Which square doesn't belong in this picture? Write the answer. ....

How many soldiers are guarding the lions' den? Write the answer. ....

MATCH THE PAIRS

Draw lines to match the identical lion pairs.

JONAH AND THE WHALE

Jonah feared God's plan for him, so he fled on his boat.
God sent a storm and Jonah was swallowed by a whale.
Find and link the letters to spell the words.

Jonah   whale   boat   storm

STORMY SEA

God saved Jonah after he promised to do God's work. Guide Jonah and the whale through the stormy sea without touching the sides.

Start →

Finish →

THE NATIVITY

Jesus was born in a stable in Bethlehem. Shepherds and wise men came to visit Him. Search the nativity scene for the things below.

How many can you see?
Write the answers in the circles.

1 donkey   .... shepherds   .... wise men

.... angels

.... sheep

.... stars

FEEDING THE 5,UUU

Crowds came to hear Jesus speak God's Word. He performed a miracle and fed all the people with only a few loaves and some fish. Use color to make the pictures match.

FIND THE FISH

Circle the fish that isn't the same in each section.

THE GOUD SHMhRIThN

A man was robbed and left hurt on the road. A Samaritan was passing by and came to help. Use the grid to finish the quiz. First, read the letter and then read the number.

For example, the donkey is in square E3.

Is the camel in B2?

Yes   No

Is the palm tree in E6?

Yes   No

Is the chameleon in D1?

Yes   No

Which square is the hurt man in? Write the answer.

....

Which square is the Good Samaritan in? Write the answer.

....

What can you see in C2?

A town

A snake

A cow

A passerby

A mouse

EASTER FUN

Jesus died on a cross to save us. He rose again after three days.
Decorate the Easter egg. Then use color to finish it.

DAZZLING DOOR HANGERS

Press out the door hangers and hang them on your door.
You could share one of them with a friend.

Dear God,
Thank you for our
wonderful world.
Amen.

Dear God,
Thank you for my
sweet dreams.
Amen.

NOAH'S ARK

On the next two pages, you will find everything you need to create Noah's ark.

1 Press out the ark and stands.

2 Slot the ark into the stands to finish.

stands

1 Press out the models and stands.

2 Then slot the stands into each model.

models

stands

BIBLE CHARACTER PAIRS

How to play:

1. Press out the cards and arrange them facedown in the play area.
2. Take turns choosing two cards and turn them faceup. If the cards match, keep the pair. If they do not match, turn them back over.
3. Keep playing until you have found all the pairs. The winner is the player with the most pairs at the end.

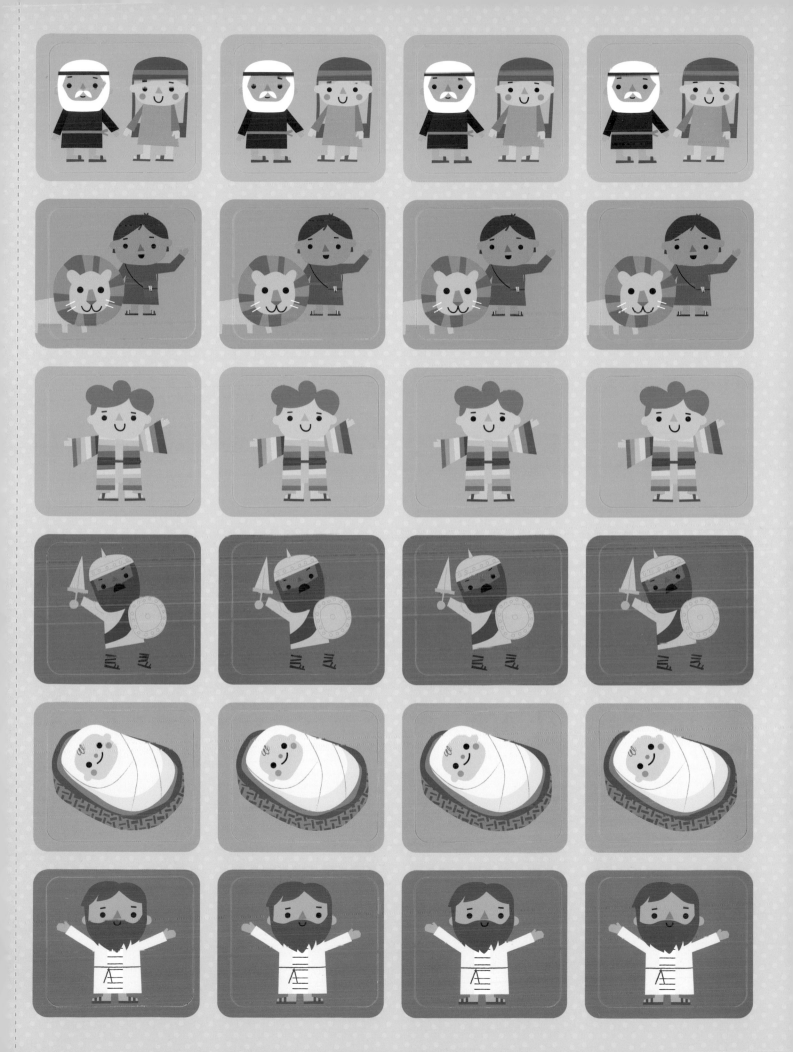

THE GOOD SHMHRITHN

1 Press out the puzzle pieces and mix them up.
2 Then put the pieces back together to make this picture.

DAVID VS GOLIATH

This is a game for 2 players.

How to play:

1 Press out the game board and counters.

2 Give one player the David counters and one player the Goliath counters.

3 Take turns putting a counter on the board. The first player to get three of their counters in a row wins!

ROAR-SOME MASK

Press out the lion mask, eye holes, and small holes either side.
Then ask an adult to help you thread some ribbon through
the small holes and tie it around your head.

JONAH'S FISH

1. Gently press out the puppet and handles.
2. Fold the puppet along the creases.
3. Glue the ends of the handles onto the back of the puppet.
4. Draw and cut out a person to be Jonah, then act out Jonah's story. Slide your hand into the puppet handles, then open and close your hand to swallow Jonah and spit him back out!

handles